I0054050

GO for IT

8

TOP

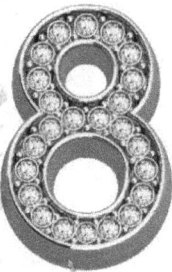

THINGS YOU
NEED TO DO TO
ACHIEVE YOUR
DREAMS

JAMEKA MORRISON-JEFFERIES

WP
WALTON
PUBLISHING HOUSE

Walton Publishing House

Copyright © 2022 by Jameka Morrison-Jefferies

All rights reserved. In accordance with the U.S. Copyright Act of 1976, the scanning, uploading, and

electronic sharing of any part of the book without the permission of the publisher constitute unlawful piracy and theft of the author's intellectual property. If you would like to use material from the book (other than for review purposes), prior written permission must be obtained by contacting the publisher at admin@iamsherriewalton.com.

Reviewers may quote brief passages in reviews.

Walton Publishing House
Houston, Texas
www.waltonpublishinghouse.com

Printed in the United States of America

Disclaimer: The advice found within may not be suitable for every individual. This work is purchased with the understanding that neither the author nor the publisher are held responsible for any results. Neither author nor publisher assumes responsibility for errors, omissions, or contrary interpretations of the subject matter herein. Any perceived disparagement of an individual or organization is a misinterpretation.

Brand and product names mentioned are trademarks that belong solely to their respective owners.

Library of Congress Cataloging-in-Publication Data under

ISBN: 978-1-953993-60-1 (digital)

         978-1-953993-61-8 (paperback)

ACKNOWLEDGEMENTS

First and foremost, I have to thank my Lord and Savior Jesus Christ for pointing me in the right direction during some of my deepest times of lack and despair. Your voice led me through countless dark days but the rewards of resilience far outweigh them all!

Next, I'd like to thank my husband Victor for allowing me to be me! Your love, support, presence, and ability to help me see the "other side" of things have been invaluable.

Special thanks to my mother, Lula M. Morrison, the absolute best cook in the world; I thank God that He has afforded me the opportunity to still have you in my life for many years.

Thank you to my early mentors in real estate: Carol Cangiano who, by divine providence, happened upon me in a coffee shop while I was still in real estate school and gave me an opportunity to learn best practices, and to Aileen Defeo, I thank you for your leadership and guidance early on in my career, for seeing the "Rock Star" realtor that I would later become, and for being a shoulder to cry on during personal challenges.

Finally, I want to give a great BIG thank you to all of my teachers, trainers, and coaches that I've had along the way, those in my inner circle, and those that have mentored me via social media. I say thank you, thank you, thank you for giving me the tools, the skills, and the fortitude to rise above every obstacle and "Go For It!"

TABLE OF CONTENTS

INTRODUCTION

With all of the voices on television, radio, podcasts, Facebook and Instagram lives, YouTube videos, and the like, I would like to personally thank you for choosing this book. I congratulate you for taking the time and responsibility of reading a manuscript that is going to give you step-by-step instructions on how to move from whatever position you find yourself in today to exactly where you see yourself in your tomorrow.

Regardless of how rocky your journey has been, you have the power to ensure that the next five years are not like the last five years. You and you alone control the trajectory of where your life leads and the velocity at which you travel. It is your God-given birthright to have, do, and be anything you desire. However, you must begin to transform your mind, your belief system, and your attitude about who you are and what you are to become. You must move from a victim mentality to a victor mentality.

There is greatness on the inside of you that you may have only seen small glimpses of but it is still there. It is now time for you to mine the untapped diamonds and precious jewels that reside inside of you. The pressure, disappointments, pain, and frustration have all played a part in you getting to this place of discovering and uncovering the true potential that you possess. If you were comfortable with your current circumstances, you wouldn't be reading this now.

The fact is, YOU WANT MORE!!! You are no longer satisfied with mediocrity and just getting by, you want ABUNDANCE! I am here to tell you that YOU CAN HAVE IT! You literally can move past your limitations, which are just your limiting beliefs, and enter into a whole new world of possibilities at this very moment.

If you are ready to receive, there is life within the pages of this book. I'm going to share with you what your teachers didn't teach you, what your coaches didn't coach you, what your parents didn't tell you, and unfortunately, what your pastors didn't share with you either. We shouldn't blame them; a lot of times people can't share what they don't know. However, now you will be without excuse because you will have a detailed outline of how to "Go For It!"

A DOUBLE-MINDED MAN IS UNSTABLE IN ALL HIS WAYS.

JAMES 1:8

1

DECISION

What do you want? Do you know most people don't *get* what they want because they don't know *what* they want? And why is that? Where did this confusion come from? Many of us as little children would go for the things that we wanted, sometimes ad nauseum. We believed that we could accomplish anything, but somewhere down the line in life, there was a disconnection. It could have been a teacher, coach, parent, church leader, spouse, family member, health crisis, or a devastating disappointment that came along to discourage you so much that it sucked the life out of you. Whatever it was, I am saying to you that it's time to heal. It's time to revisit your heart's desires, and believe in yourself again. Yet to do so, you must make a decision.

By its very definition, a decision means to draw a conclusion to make a final choice or judgment about. But if you take time to study the word a little further and understand the root of the word, you'll see there is an even deeper spiritual esoteric meaning. In Latin, the word is *decidere* which means to "cut off;" so, in essence, when you make a decision, you are cutting off any other possible outcomes outside of what it is you have decided upon.

I heard Dr. Myron Golden explain that a decision is a cut or an incision, a covenant much like what circumcision was in the Old Testament between God and Abraham. It signifies that you are in agreement with whatever you righteously want to possess and it has spiritual implications when you decide upon a thing.

So, my friends, it is utterly important that you become definite with the infinite and begin to get real with yourself not about what you think is the "politically correct" thing to want, for example, world peace. Although that is a great and noble desire, if you are honest with yourself that is not what you truly want. Most of you want M.O.R.E.

- » More Money
- » Overflow
- » Residuals
- » Excess

Let us begin to break this down for a moment. Ecclesiastes 10:19 says "*Money answereth all things.*" My acronym M.O.R.E. stands for the exact reason why I had to change my mindset concerning what I truly wanted and needed more of, MONEY. I am a Christian businesswoman and that is who I am at my very core, but I have to be honest, my epiphany came at the time of this publication roughly 1,100 days ago.

It was a hot summer night when I attended a tent revival and "we had church." But after it was over, I said to myself, "There has to be more than this!" My thoughts became extremely inquisitive, and I began to ask God some questions right there. I asked, "Lord, where are the signs and where are the wonders?" What I was really asking was, *"Where are the wonders in my life?"*

Sure, I was a successful realtor at the time and I managed to make a "decent" living. My husband and I took our trips and bought our toys but it wasn't what Jesus promised in John 10:10 which was life *MORE* abundantly. I saw not enough, and I saw just enough but I was looking for *El Shaddai*, which in Hebrew means "more than enough."

Suddenly, it hit me! I heard God speak back to me and say, "You're not doing it right." I was floored and I responded, "Well Lord, I'm faithful. I go to church and pay my tithes." What happened next changed my life for almost three years and shot me into the stratosphere. He said, "You've been doing *church* stuff and you've been doing *religious* stuff but you haven't been doing *Kingdom* stuff!" Whoa, that blew my mind! That was the day I made a decision to go on a quest as stated in Matthew 6:33, KJV *"But seek ye first the Kingdom of God, and his righteousness; and all these <u>things</u> will be added unto you."*

Boy, did I get excited! It was like I had taken off on a new adventure for knowledge, truth, and understanding and I began to fall in love with the word of God again! It was amazing because I understood that when I began to see what this new world was about, I had to learn, unlearn, and relearn the truth about who I was and what I was entitled to on this earth, and not just when I get to Heaven.

A world of endless possibilities unveiled itself as if a curtain of awesomeness was suddenly displayed to me in new and exciting ways. Unexpectedly, I started to believe it was possible for ME! What if I could drive what I want to drive, live where I want to live, and express myself at my highest, most successful self without any limitations? I had to get delivered from people and their opinions of me (we'll discuss more about this in other chapters). This is not just for me, but you too can find freedom by learning the principles that are presented throughout the various chapters of this book.

Rev. Frederick Eikerenkoetter describes visualization as entering into the *theater of your mind and the stage of your imagination*. Once I caught on to this concept and put it into practice, all bets were off and it was GO TIME! I was fascinated with my own self-discovery. I began to take time out to discuss with myself the desires I had. A decision had to be made but I had to make it for myself- no one could do it for me. The same applies to you.

It is not selfish for you to begin to put yourself first, it's necessary. Make a daily concerted effort to put the spotlight back on yourself before you can help anyone else. This concept may seem foreign to you because you have been bending over backward for years, pleasing other people and looking for approval from others. Introspection as defined by Merriam-Webster.com is "an observation or examination of one's mental and emotional processes." When was the last time you asked yourself, "how are *you* doing today?"

Reflection must become the compass by which you navigate your daily activities. You have to be mindful of what's important to you and keep your gaze fixed on it continuously. A decision has to be made, if not now, when? If not me, who? The only one that can change the conditions that you are presently in is *Y-O-U*!

Self-discovery will lead to self-mastery; self-mastery leads to high self-esteem. When you feel good about yourself, others will feel good about you as well and that's when the *Magic Happens*! It would be as if a light bulb has been illuminated within you and all will see it, and be drawn to it. The beauty in this is new people will be drawn to you, and these new relationships will prove to be mutually beneficial in several ways including:

» Future revenue for your business.

» Ideas that can help you level up.

» Specialized knowledge that you can glean from and duplicate their success.

One decision can change your financial future landscape. Do you know what that means? Let me share a quick story.

I decided I wanted to branch out into luxury real estate sales, so I purchased a course to learn about luxury real estate and how to break into the industry. I traveled to attend the seminar in Tampa, Florida, to meet with the CEO of a top-producing real estate brokerage featured on a hit television show on Netflix filmed there. I arrived in Tampa on a late flight, and I was exhausted. The next morning my body wanted to rest up and skip the Chamber of Commerce event on real estate, but something happened. My goal of breaking into luxury real estate flashed before me, and I sat straight up in the bed, looked over at my husband, and said, "I have to go!" I put on my fire-red dress and headed out the door driving thirty long, agonizing minutes to the venue.

Upon arrival, I proceeded to the registration table and took my seat in the room. I wasn't impressed, to say the least. The seminar speakers were dry and off-topic. There were two "chatterboxes" sitting next to me that talked the entire day. I was beyond aggravated by the time the event was almost over when a middle-aged tanned gentleman with gleaming white teeth and old Hollywood good looks stood up and walked to my table. He randomly sat down next to me, after a few minutes, we both started chatting. We discovered that we were both in real estate. He was also a luxury real estate broker with a very high-level brokerage firm. Out of nowhere, he asked me if I would help him sell a 2.8-million-dollar waterfront property on the shoreline! Of course, I said yes, but that's not where the story ends.

One of the event speakers was an executive from Jaigantic Studios, a movie and television production company created by film and action movie star, Michael Jai White. He had recently moved back to Connecticut from Hollywood. The executive and I talked for a bit and then a handsome young gentleman walked in. Upon being introduced to this dazzling young executive with an infectious smile, the young man turned to me and said, "I know you! You used to be a personal trainer at the gym I attended, and you were always looking fabulous!" The executive informed me the young man was Devin White, Michael Jai White's son! I was flabbergasted and dumbfounded by the encounter. What were the chances of him knowing who I was? I had never seen him before in my life.

What happened next is even more mind-blowing because he then revealed that they were looking for location scouts to help them find homes and buildings in various locations for their film and T.V. projects. Kaboom! What a mind-blowing moment!!! I introduced him to my new 2.8-million-dollar guy! Serendipity was at work because we all met at that event to make the deal happen! That was a lesson in perseverance. I learned to keep pushing through fatigue, doubt, fear, or whatever may attempt to hold me back. We never know what greatness awaits on the other side of it!

The late Bob Proctor said on his YouTube channel, "You've got to make a committed decision. You're going to have to do it regardless. Let no one decide for you, it's your life!" Again, I reiterate, you must become very transparent about what you truly, earnestly want and desire. No one will judge you because you will tell no one; it's just you and God in the room. Do you want a Bentley, Lamborghini, or a Subaru? I don't care what it is, just be honest about it with no-holds-barred.

Do you want to be in a relationship again? Maybe you've been burned, scorned, or physically, mentally, or financially abused by a past companion and you're afraid to trust again. However, you know deep down in your heart you want another relationship. Go ahead and write it down. This is a safe place where you can reacquaint yourself with yourself. Find out who you are and become that person you once dreamed you could be.

I usually have my students take out a sheet of paper and write 100 goals down. I encourage you to do that right now, just begin to let the pen flow freely and feel how good it feels to dream again. This is between you and your maker, no one has to know how ostentatious or grandiose they may be.

Keep your aspirations close to your vest as they say. Sometimes when you share your newfound joy and your paradigm begins to shift, your "well-meaning" friends and family may want to "talk some sense" into you! Don't listen to them! Remember the folks that have helped you get to where you are now probably won't be the ones that take you to the next level.

One last word on decision-making. I have had the pleasure of coaching and mentoring folks all around the country, ages 18-80 and the question I always ask is "what do you want out of life?" I am always so shocked by their answers. An overwhelming 95% of them often say "I don't know." That's like walking into McDonald's and when the server asks, may I take your order please, you stand there mumbling uh, um, uh... Do you know gets annoyed with you? It's not just the person who's standing there waiting on you, but also the other people standing in line behind you waiting for you to make a decision!

People, the world is waiting for you to fulfill your purpose so that they can be beneficiaries of what you produce!

Affirmation:

I am so thankful and grateful to God that I am making decisions for my future that will positively affect me and the world I live in.

Commence pouring out your deepest most innermost desires before Him and commit them in writing on paper. Personally, I keep a digital and a handwritten goal journal. How else will you know what to go for, if you don't know what you're going for?

Use the space below to write down your top 10 goals. These are the areas that you would love to see come to fruition in your life within the next 1, 5, or even 10 years from now. You'll be surprised at how good you'll feel once you commit them to paper and more importantly when you get to cross them off and make new ones.

GO FOR IT

1. _____
   _____
   _____
   _____
   _____

2. _____
   _____
   _____
   _____
   _____

3. _____
   _____
   _____
   _____
   _____

4. _____
   _____
   _____
   _____
   _____

5. _____
   _____
   _____
   _____
   _____

6. _____
_____
_____
_____
_____

7. _____
_____
_____
_____
_____

8. _____
_____
_____
_____
_____

9. _____
_____
_____
_____
_____

10. _____
_____
_____
_____
_____

"

JESUS SAID UNTO HIM, IF THOU CANST BELIEVE, ALL THINGS ARE POSSIBLE TO HIM THAT BELIEVETH.

MARK 9:23 KJV

"

2

BELIEF AND AFFIRMATION SYSTEM

What is your belief about yourself? Do you believe you deserve the best? Do you believe you're worthy of the best life has to offer? These questions are crucial in identifying your inability to rise above low self-esteem issues that cause you to self-sabotage any glimpse of success that may be attempting to spring forth in your life.

Your belief system, or what you've been hearing referred to lately from all of the self-help personal development gurus, as your paradigm, is the nucleus of which you must resolve to dismantle and rebuild at once! Your belief system is the essence of what makes you, you.

If you don't make a concerted daily effort to transform your current beliefs into what is actually the truth about you, success will elude you. However, if you will adopt the habits that are detailed in this book, you will inevitably see your dreams materialize in astonishing ways.

Steps to implement your new-belief-system strategy:

1. Come to the realization that you can have, do, and be anything that you want to have, do, and be. Remember, if you want what you never had, you must do what you've never done. That means becoming radical for change. The current belief system has gotten you the results you have today, so what do you have to lose? It's imperative that you commence using these next steps at once. Success loves speed and you must get in gear!

2. Now that you've written your goals, begin to idealize what your dream life looks like. Imagine how your ideal self looks.

    What are you wearing?

    Where are you living?

    How does your home look?

What type of car(s) are you driving?

How much are you earning per year?

3. Become mindful of your thoughts. Guard them and refuse to let anything or anyone speak to you negatively. You are also not allowed to think or speak negatively about yourself. Regardless of what has taken place prior to today, the past is in the past, you are a new person acquiring new skills. The fact that you are this far into this book suggests that you want more. Your tenacity to complete the task this time must be on full throttle.

4. Turn the television off and stop reading newspapers or checking gossip websites.

5. Refuse to be distracted by flashy headlines designed to draw you into their world of shootings, murders, recessions, wars, kidnappings, and the like. You are formulating a new world of positivity around you. A world filled with yes, abundance, progress, overflow, fruitfulness, and joy!

6. Find a mentor. If you don't know of any currently, look for mentors in your hometown. If there are none, find a virtual mentor.

Surround yourself with positive people at all costs. Disassociate yourself from old acquaintances that merely want to discuss negative events in the world; those who want to have old conversations about nothing. Distance yourself, limit yourself and if at all possible, cut them off until your self-imposed mind transformation is complete.

Distancing yourself may seem harsh, but it is necessary to pull away for a period of time to get YOU together. If they love you, they will allow you the space required for you to train and develop your skills for growth and wealth preparation, if not, they were never in your corner in the first place. In the long run, you'll be more of a resource from a position of power than from a position of lack and want.

The adoption of the previous instructions and strict adherence is essential to your success. Just like getting in better shape requires you to exercise and go "cold turkey" from sugar and fatty fried foods for the best results, the same is true for "innercise." John Assaraf's wrote about this mentality training in his book, Innercise: The New Science to Unlock Your Brain's Hidden Power. If this is a new term for you, innercise means that you place just as much emphasis on working out your mind as you do working out your physical body.

Innercise means training your mind to focus on exactly what you want it to think, visualizing exactly how you see your future and refusing to accept any outcome that is contrary to you receiving all of the good this life has to offer you. You must powerwash your brain from the garbage of old bad teachings, bad advice, bad habits, and conversations you had with bad company over the past 20, 30, or maybe even 50 plus years! This includes dismantling the unproductive dialogue you've had with well-meaning, overprotective parents over the years.

Unhealthy conversations come in many forms. Maybe you were in foster care with uncaring abusive foster parents who looked at you as a meal ticket. Perhaps there was a coach or teacher who took out their frustrations of not becoming a world-renowned best-selling author. Maybe a pro-athlete lashed out and attempted to berate you because of their inadequacies. It could have been a religious leader that attempted to dash your hopes of becoming a speaker or minister because you were a woman and you challenged them in bible study and they wanted to suppress your gifts by "sitting you down."

Whatever your story is, you no longer have to be a victim of word curses from nay-sayers. You have the last say in how your life turns out. You are in control of how and what you think. This principle is what many motivational mindset gurus, speakers, coaches, trainers, and authors rely on. They support my previous claims of mental liberty and clarity from all previous negative statements ever spoken over you. The Bible mentions this as well in Proverbs 23:7, "Whatsoever a man thinks in his heart, so is he."

You may be asking, *is it really just as simple as thinking of myself the way I want to be, and I don't need anyone else's agreement or validation?* The answer is yes, it really is just that simple. But although it's simple, it's not easy. It takes work to develop a new mindset but it will be worth it in the long run. Viktor E. Frankl, bestselling author, neurologist, psychiatrist, and holocaust survivor credited his survival to learning to control his thoughts. No matter what he faced or what his circumstances were presumed to be, i.e., exposure to cold, nakedness, and even hunger, the Nazis could not control his thoughts! In one of his speeches, he is quoted as saying, "If we take man as he is, we make him worse, but if we take man as what he should be, we make him capable of becoming what he can be." That, my friends, is one's belief in their future self, not their present condition.

What are some of the limiting beliefs that you currently have? Take some time to identify some of the negative, non-edifying thoughts and phrases you've told yourself over the years.

Examples of this are statements like:

» I'm not good enough.

» I don't have enough education.

» I'm too old.

» I'm too young.

» I'm not handsome/pretty enough.

» I don't speak well.

» No one in my family ever did that, so I could never afford that.

» I could never live there.

» These are the cards that I've been dealt.

Take some time and jot down at least 10 negative self-defeating thoughts you have had about yourself:

1. _____
   _____
   _____
   _____
   _____

2. _____
   _____
   _____
   _____
   _____

3. _____
   _____
   _____
   _____
   _____

4. _____
   _____
   _____
   _____
   _____

5. _____
   _____
   _____
   _____
   _____

6. _____
_____
_____
_____
_____
_____

7. _____
_____
_____
_____
_____
_____

8. _____
_____
_____
_____
_____
_____

9. _____
_____
_____
_____
_____
_____

10. _____
_____
_____
_____
_____

Now that you've completed that exercise, you are going to replace those negative ideas, misconceptions, and perceptions with affirmations stating the opposite. You may feel like, hey, that's lying. But it's not. It is normal to feel that way when you're re-engineering your thought processes about yourself. What you are experiencing is your logical conscious mind speaking to you.

However, what you are doing is what I've coined "predictive programming." This is the act of speaking the truth of all the good that you wish to do, to have, and to be in the present tense and acting as if it is already done.

You are going to speak the exact opposite of what your negative thoughts suggested. Below are some examples to help you get started.

Negative Thought #1: I am not good enough.

Positive Affirmation: I am good enough; I am better today than I was yesterday.

Negative Thought #2: I don't have enough education.

Positive Affirmation: I am learning new things every day. I am educating myself daily.

When you use predictive programming, you speak directly to your subconscious mind which does not know the difference between what's true and what *will be* true. I love working with the subconscious mind because this is the heart of a person. This is where your true, most inner-self, lies. This is where your ideal self can take shape and form if you make direct and deliberate actions to train it regularly on a daily basis.

When should you practice this predictive programming? I have found the best times are first thing in the morning when you are in what neuro-scientists call an "alpha" state and right before bed. This is typically when your conscious mind begins to wind down. Brian Tracy, one of the world's most recognized authorities on goal-setting calls this form of communicating with one's self "Back From The Future Thinking." This is where you see your future self already in possession of all of the skills, money, and knowledge that you desire.

> *"Therefore I say unto you, what things soever ye desire when ye pray, believe that ye receive them, and ye shall have them."*
> (MARK 11:24 KJV)

When I committed this scripture to memory, my life changed in some of the most miraculous ways because I didn't just remember and recite it, I internalized, emotionalized, and believed in it! Seeing is freeing!

I will now introduce you to the second most important step in your quest for fulfillment and enjoyment in your life - visualization.

"

WHERE THERE IS NO VISION, THE PEOPLE PERISH.

PROVERBS 29:18 KJV

"

3

VISUALIZATION

Every morning, take 6-10 luxuriating breaths and immediately begin to practice thankfulness for being alive. My favorite thing to do after meditating is visualizing. Your blueprint for what to visualize is based on the goals you wrote down in the preceding chapters. This is where you see yourself in possession of, in the place of, in the body of the person you ideally want to be. Napoleon Hill said in his self-help book in 1937 *Think and Grow Rich,* "Whatever your mind can conceive and believe, it can achieve." Become so enveloped and engrossed in your vision that you have the very minute details etched into your subconscious mind.

If you wrote down that you want a new home, see the new home in your mind. Envision details like:

» What color is it?

» How many bedrooms/baths does it have?

» What state or country is it in?

» How many acres does it sit on?

» How many square feet is it?

Do you get the point? You must visualize the details down to the appliances, the flooring, the swimming pool, the tennis courts, etc. Do you have pets? What are their names? Call their names in your vision; you are free to see whatever comes into your heart and mind. Make your vision extremely vivid and see yourself in your home laughing, enjoying yourself, and helping yourself to all of the delicious food in your newly designed chef's kitchen. Visualize what clothing you are wearing; what's the weather like; is the wind blowing? The more detailed you are, the more God and the laws and principles in the realm of the spiritual have to work with to attract these things to you.

> *"For the vision is yet for an appointed time, but at the end it shall speak and not lie. Though it tarry, wait for it, because it will surely come; it will not tarry."*
>
> **(HABAKKUK 2:3 KJV)**

> *"What you are thinking right now is a future goal. But guess what? It may not happen tomorrow, but it's certainly coming. Be patient, it will not delay."*
>
> **JAMEKA'S TRANSLATION**

The encouragement that this scripture offers is invaluable. It deals with settling the mental tennis match that happens after you decide you are going to implement a new way of approaching your everyday life. Whenever you make a drastic change that causes a pattern interruption in your previous monotonous routine, opposition to those plans tend to show up. Why? Because that part of your brain called the amygdala that is designed to keep you "safe" from disappointment, danger, and discouragement wants to talk you out of taking a chance. It serves its purpose; it keeps you from making potentially harmful mistakes like stepping out into traffic or getting into a stranger's car.

However, when it comes to you realizing your potential and getting you to your next dimension in life, you have to work to suppress its influence on your conscious and subconscious mind. That part of your brain wants you to think that delay is denial. It tricks you into believing that just because what you prayed for, believed for, and sacrificed for didn't happen right away means it's not going to happen.

Nothing could be further from the truth. Because it hasn't happened yet is a testament that it will happen! I know that's a mind twister but here's the thing about "becoming" - it takes time. A good cook doesn't become a great cook overnight, it takes a few burned cakes, a couple of "not so great" recipes, and a whole lot of trial and error "before" they become a renowned chef. You can't give up. Continue to see yourself standing triumphantly in your area of expertise and you will be that person!

If you are praying prayers that start with "Lord, whatever you give me...." Stop! It is not God's will that you pray that way. I know you are probably shocked that I would make such a controversial assertion because all prayer is acceptable, but you are God's highest creation and He does not want you just to get by and accept whatever life gives you. In Isaiah 45:11, God implicitly says to His people "Command Ye Me!" That means be specific, be intentional, and be unwavering in your request, boldly in confidence. As I heard Rev. Ike say, "Be definite with the infinite." Again, most people don't get what they want because they *don't know* what they want.

I attended a family gathering recently and decided to test my theory. I took a poll, and I asked one person after the next, "What do you like to do? What do you want to do? When do you want to do it?" I was met with one blank stare after another only to conclude the unanimous answer was an resounding "I don't know." To be successful you must have a plan. The good news for you though, after completing the exercises at the end of the chapter, you will have a plan. You will know, and not just know, but you will be equipped to GO!

There are no shortcuts, you have to do the work. I heard someone once say, "All work, works. It's either working for you or it's working on you." Your responsibility is to continue to do the necessary work that it will take for you to improve your mental acuity, your success mindset, and your business acumen. It will all work out for you in the end, I promise.

Visualization requires a serious discipline of the mind, much like prayer. Allow me to explain what I mean. Have you ever set out to pray and found it difficult to do because all of a sudden you get hungry, or you start wondering about what you're going to eat? Your mind wanders and thinks about if you left the stove on or what errands you have to run. I am pretty sure this has happened to you on more than one occasion. Visualization can be interrupted in the same manner. You must, at all costs, redirect your thoughts back to what you are imagining. Don't allow exasperation to win; as with anything it takes practice. Be patient with yourself as you begin to experiment with this new daily routine. Take your time and work with your visualization. This is a proven tool that will cement your goals and dreams into your subconscious mind. Your ability to create the picture in your mind will manifest the tangible riches and successes that you seek.

It's the principle found in Proverbs 23:7, "Whatsoever a man thinketh in his heart so is he," is real!

» Meditation/Prayer/Thankfulness

» Visualizing/Emotionalizing

» Journaling

» Reading - Inspirational Manuscripts, Exercise

» Take Action - Get Up/Go Out/Meet Life/Make Moves

In 2018, at the inception of my mindset transformation, I wanted a new futuristic motorcycle called a Slingshot. It has 3 wheels, it drives like a car, and it was for lack of a better phrase, super sexy! While I was driving my four-door Lexus, I envisioned that my car was my Slingshot. I felt the engine roar. I could feel the wind on my face. I saw my hair blowing in the wind- it was all so vivid and it felt real. During that time, I began carrying an index card in my pocket and I looked at it every day and spoke out loud as I read the index card, "I Drive a Slingshot!" I exclaimed. I put the words in the present tense and not in the past tense. I didn't say, "I am going to," or "I will be" it was "I drive."

When you emotionalize you must operate in the present tense because the subconscious mind will make it future tense. The subconscious mind only recognizes NOW and then it gets to work making sure it comes to pass. I held on to that card, and visualization and emotionalization became a daily disciple. In 2020 Polaris revealed the first automatic Slingshot in history! Coincidence, I think not! I drove to the dealership ready to purchase my Slingshot. After preparing my credit and working on my financial discipline I was met with good news,

"Mrs. Jefferies we hardly ever see anyone come in here with credit as good as yours. You don't have to put down any money and your interest rate is super low," said the salesman.

Yes, it was a dream come true. Now before you pass judgment on me and say that's great but that's a liability Jameka, I turned it into an asset and we rent it out on Turo, cha-ching!

This next example felt like nothing short of a miracle, because after a seemingly short period of time of putting these strategic actions into practice something beautiful happened. One day, during the reading exploration phase of my morning ritual, I was led to Bob Proctor's YouTube video on mindset. In the video he described something so outlandish and outrageous I couldn't believe my ears. He very confidently said, "Do you know that you can make all that you made in one year in one month?" I was floored, I had never thought or heard of anything as elaborate as that before! Initially, it was difficult to wrap my mind around that idea, however, the optimist in me, started to believe that it was possible, and not only was it possible, but it was also possible for me!

I quickly began to work on myself and I started to believe in greater. Up until that time, the most I had made in one year was $30,000. I began to say in my affirmations, "I earn $30,000 per month." The next year, my income doubled. The following year it increased again. But then something amazing happened in year three - my income quadrupled and we began averaging $20-25,000 per month. Supernatural? Absolutely! Previously, the old me had a financial thermostat stuck between $30-60,000K per year. Hearing and believing more was possible for me shifted the trajectory of my life.

I will always be thankful for entrepreneurs who come along and share their experiences of overcoming to help others, like myself, shake loose from childhood phobias. Growing up I had a fear of success. Every time I started to get ahead I would self-sabotage and stop. After years of self-discovery, I now know that internally I didn't believe I deserved more even though I wanted more.

My other discovery was that I had impostor syndrome. I believed I was succeeding in life sometimes by accident. I found sales success early in my career, selling advertising for the cable company in my state. I have memories of accomplishing the recognition of the number one sales rep in the country of a Fortune 500 company. As a reward for my accomplishment, I treated myself to a trip to the Bahamas. I was 25 years old, single and the world was my oyster.

While I was there having a great time in Nassau, I received a call in my hotel room from my co-worker back in the States telling me that everyone in my department was fired and/or laid off. Shocked and bewildered by the news I returned to work with all of the corporate brass standing around my desk saying don't worry, your job is *safe* and we want you to stay and take all of the accounts. What they were offering me was a management position in the sales department. As a perk, the company offered to give me stock options, but I had no idea what stock options were. What should I do? I asked myself. Call it survivor's remorse, fear of success, or whatever but I retreated to a familiar place, where I felt safe.

A co-worker and friend asked me to come over to where all of my ex-co-workers had moved to, the competitor. Truth be told, I moved because I wanted to prove to myself that I was good enough and that being number one at my previous company wasn't a fluke. I needed to know if I could duplicate my success at another company in a territory far from where anyone knew me. Guess what? I was right, I did it again and achieved AT&T's Sales Rookie of the year. However, the success was short-lived because no matter how well I did I couldn't shake the feelings of inadequacy that I still harbored. I had to be renewed in the spirit of my mind and transformed which unfortunately took me years to realize. However, I've got it now!

What I learned from all of that is when you don't see yourself as a successful winner inside it will be impossible to keep up appearances on the outside. Visualization gives you the mental capacity to see the coming attraction before the movie plays out. Often those who practice this method regularly have stated that because they have played the scene of what they expect so often, when it actually happens it is no surprise. They've been preparing for it mentally days, weeks, and months prior!

Images in your mind are powerful and that is why whatever image you have of yourself must be that of a successful, wealthy, healthy, well-balanced individual because what you see is what you get. Begin today, begin now! Take a moment and stop what you're doing and envision in your mind's eye, who and what you want to become; be him or her right now for 60 seconds.

Take a moment to write down what you saw in the recesses of your mind in your visualization:

1. _____
   _____
   _____
   _____
   _____

2. _____
   _____
   _____
   _____
   _____

3. _____
   _____
   _____
   _____
   _____

4. _____
   _____
   _____
   _____
   _____

5. _____
   _____
   _____
   _____
   _____

6. _____

_____

_____

_____

_____

7. _____

_____

_____

_____

_____

8. _____

_____

_____

_____

_____

9. _____

_____

_____

_____

_____

10. _____

_____

_____

_____

_____

**EMOTIONS ARE
ENERGY IN MOTION**

—————

JOHN BRADSHAW
WWW.RELATIONSHIPENRICHMENT.COM

4

EMOTIONALIZING

Have you read the book or seen the movie *The Secret* and still came away feeling as though the information was still, in fact, a secret? Many people indeed have felt that way and just could not grasp the fact that a person could literally think their way into happiness, prosperity, better health, and overall, just a better way of life. When I first read it many years ago, I must admit I too let my skepticism impede my willingness to consistently adopt the principles that were taught in the book. I attribute this to my belief that because neither my pastor, nor my mother, nor my teachers had taught me this stuff, it can't be true. Well, not only did I discover that all of it was true but the one component that could've propelled me farther and faster with better results was this one little missing factor which was "Emotionalizing." This means that all I had to do was meditate, visualize the ideal scenario that I wanted for my life and then "FEEL IT!" Yes, you read that correctly.

Although it may have been touched on briefly in the movie and book, not enough emphasis was placed on the actual embodiment of already being in possession of whatever your desired outcome is. The way this looks is you begin to attach some of the greatest feelings you've ever had of achievement i.e.: purchasing your first home, getting a promotion, or winning a coveted award. What about being proposed to by the person of your dreams? Whatever that high-achieving feeling is, bring it into your visualization and bask in it.

Here's an example of a dream car visualization and several questions you should ask yourself while you are emotionally visualizing:

1. How do I feel while I'm driving my dream car?
2. What am I wearing while driving my dream car?
3. Who else is there with me?
4. What's the weather like? Is the sun shining? How does this make you feel?
5. What does this car signify to you? Is it wealth or a sense of accomplishment? Do you feel like you have finally achieved success?

Take the time to define the "why," and what that particular accomplishment will mean to you once you get It. Be honest about your desires and reasoning behind them. This is a part of becoming the true, authentic you.

Another issue that I found that keeps people back from pursuing and achieving their dreams is worrying about what other people will think about them. I met a young lady who was working on a cruise ship and we were talking about goals and she said that since she got her good job and is able to travel the world, people in her hometown accuse her of "thinking" she is all that and better than them. Isn't it interesting that no one accuses you of those things when you're suffering alongside them? No longer will you meander through life with people-pleasing motives. This book is about positioning you into a place of freedom to be, do and have what YOU want, not anyone else!

The only person you need to convince about becoming everything you can be is *yourself*. Emotion is energy in motion, therefore put all of your energy into your goals and plans for you and your family. Refuse to be side-tracked by the distraction and noise in your own head. Now I must warn you. When you begin this intensive intentional meditation and emotional visualization you will begin to see that random thoughts will show up, this is normal, simply acknowledge they are there but get right back to your goals and plans, and see them already accomplished. You may ask, Jameka, how long does it take for these things to come to fruition? My answer is, instead of asking how long, ask how often? The more you feel it, the more it happens!

Right now, take a moment to jot down 10 things that you are going to implement today to get you to feel emotionally better about yourself:

1. _____
   _____
   _____
   _____
   _____

2. _____
   _____
   _____
   _____
   _____

3. _____
   _____
   _____
   _____
   _____

4. _____
   _____
   _____
   _____
   _____

5. _____
   _____
   _____

6.

7.

8.

9.

10.

AND THE LORD ANSWERED ME AND SAID, " WRITE THE VISION, AND MAKE IT PLAIN UPON TABLES, THAT HE MAY RUN THAT READETH IT.

HABAKKUK 2:2 NKJV

5

JOURNALING

The best way to start your journal is with one simple action that anyone can do and that's with simple reflection. Being grateful and thankful in your journal really sets the tone for your day. Think about it, how difficult would it be to wake up on the wrong side of the bed when you're thankful for everything as soon as you open your eyes? You are to use this time first thing in the morning to reflect on what went well the day before. The truth is, the more you give thanks, the more things you will have to be thankful for. It's amazing how that works. It is incredibly mind-blowing to discover just how things will begin to turn around for you when you meet life with optimism and enthusiasm. Life will meet you, as you meet life.

In other words, you are tracking your progress as you soldier on towards the successful outcome that you long for and desire. It is time out for you not having specifics and details about the structure and overall design of the exact result you have etched into your imagination. The late great Jim Rohn once said in one of his amazing thought-provoking speeches:

> *"The best time to build is when it's finished!"*

Wow, how true those words are. You have to begin with the end in *mind*, and how do you best do that? You have to put it on paper, map out the schematics, and with faith, fortitude, and resilience start building. Get to work journaling/ tracking/ documenting your vision and focusing on the "what" and the "why" and leave the "how" up to the Master. You may have heard the phrase; the devil is in the details. Well, I believe, the blessing is in the details. When it comes to framing out your lifestyle design, the more detailed you are the more likely you will see it come to fruition. Being precise with laser-focused descriptions of what it is you want is not just a suggestion, it is a command.

When a builder sets out to create what the architect has sketched out and designed on paper, he doesn't say, "I think I'll just cut this wood beam maybe a half-inch thick," or "I'm guessing it will be about 2 feet long." No, he has to have precise measurements. Not only for the building to look right aesthetically but also for it to stand erect and not collapse. Every detail, every measurement, and every plan have to be followed to the letter for a "quality" product to last and sustain weather conditions of all kinds and overall wear and tear over the years.

The same is true with journaling; precise details have to be written in order for you to see what you desire materialize. In fact, you must be so detailed that when it shows up there will be no mistaking that you were responsible for its birth. The experience takes place first mentally before it shows up physically. It is vital to write the visions in your mind down daily. Not only will this keep you laser-focused on your goals, but the written vision will act as a plan of action and a reference roadmap of success as you journey towards your glorious destination. Personally, I love being a goal-setter because I then become a goal-getter! The men and women on my team and in my training don't just learn in theory, they are also manifesters of the good they desire for themselves and their families.

The Law of Momentum states that "an object/body in motion stays in motion until acted upon by an outside force." - https://byjus.com. Once you start the journey of recalibrating your mind for success, and do it consistently for a certain amount of time, it will be difficult to revert to former self-defeating and self-deprecating habits and ways of thinking. In fact, you will lose joy in participating in old conversations with old former acquaintances because they will be stuck in the '80s, '90s, and early 2000s while you're walking around in your future!

While you are peeling off layers of your old self and becoming the *you* that you always knew yourself to be, you may face backlash from friends and family but that's okay, do not be alarmed, it is a part of the process. They will soon accept this new positive version of you or they will fall away. In either case, you will be better for it because you will be replaced with people who share the same belief system and are able to relate to you on a much higher sophisticated plane.

An example of this happened to me as I was in my earlier stage of becoming. I had a family member lash out at me and say, "You know what, you think more highly of yourself than you ought to, you need to humble yourself!" Now, this was particularly weird because if I don't think highly of myself, who will? I will not bore you with my response, but these are some of the ignorant statements that may pass through the lips of some of your former cohorts.

In any event, pay them no mind because they are just upset you are leaving the crew before they could get a clue. Harriet Tubman said, "I freed a thousand slaves.

I could have freed a thousand more if they knew they were slaves."

When it comes to journaling, you can create a written or digital one. I utilize both, although I lean more toward the written journal. Let me explain why. With all of the convenience of having a digital journal, the only drawback is that research has shown typing only allows you to use one side of your brain whereas a hand-written journal uses both sides. A great resource on understanding behaviors and how the brain works is "*Innercise: The New Science to Unlock Your Brain's Hidden Power* by John Assaraf. There is a brain/hand connection that neurologists believe is super effective in activating the Reticular Activating System (RAS) in your brain. This is truly a powerful source.

RAS, as explained by lifexchangesolutions.com, is a system controlled by neurons that travel through the neural pathways, or thoughts that get stored in your subconscious for automatic memory recall. In other words, you can train your mind through positive repetitive thoughts to see opportunities that previously were hidden from you. For example, let's say you have purchase a new red Toyota, and as soon as you leave the car dealership you begin to see red Toyotas everywhere. That is your RAS taking over!

Journaling provides a historical play-by-play account of all the wonderment you have experienced the day before or expect to experience on a daily basis. Well, you are probably asking, how can you be certain or sure something great is going to happen every day? I am telling you this because you're going to look for it. If you are actively looking for magnificent things to happen, they will, but you have to document it. Journaling is a way of documenting your successes as they will inevitably show up in awesome and magnificent ways. The key to all of what I am describing is consistency. You cannot expect to receive anything if you waver and deviate from the blueprint.

By definition, and according to Merriam-Webster.com, journaling is:

> » a record of experiences, ideas, or reflections kept regularly for private use: DIARY

> » a record of current transactions especially: a book of original entry in double-entry bookkeeping

> » an account of day-to-day events

If you would prefer a digital journal, it is effective as well. Digital journals are super accessible. Using a digital journal also allows you the flexibility and leisure of looking up a scripture or cross-referencing another manuscript all at your fingertips, day or night. You can start journaling today! Let's start now with the top 20 things you want to accomplish in 60, 90, 120, and 365 days from now!

Write down what went well for you the day before and put this into practice daily. Nothing is too hard for the power of your imagination and the God-power you have within you; LET'S GO!

GO FOR IT

1. _____
   _____
   _____
   _____
   _____

2. _____
   _____
   _____
   _____
   _____

3. _____
   _____
   _____
   _____
   _____

4. _____
   _____
   _____
   _____
   _____

5. _____
   _____
   _____
   _____
   _____

6. _____
_____
_____
_____
_____

7. _____
_____
_____
_____
_____

8. _____
_____
_____
_____
_____

9. _____
_____
_____
_____
_____

10. _____
_____
_____
_____
_____

11. _____
_____
_____
_____
_____

12. _____
_____
_____
_____
_____

13. _____
_____
_____
_____
_____

14. _____
_____
_____
_____
_____

15. _____
_____
_____
_____
_____

16. _____
_____
_____
_____
_____

17. _____
_____
_____
_____
_____

18. _____
_____
_____
_____
_____

19. _____
_____
_____
_____
_____

20. _____
_____
_____
_____
_____

FAITH WITHOUT WORKS IS DEAD.

——

JAMES 2:26 NKJV

ACTION

Once the previous steps have been implemented, it is time to take massive action on your business and life goals. What does this mean? It means you will get your plan of action and do the necessary things that will achieve your desired results and outcomes. For instance, if you want to move into a new industry or change your job or career, you must begin to focus all of your attention on that idea. Your value to the marketplace must increase exponentially and the only way to increase your value after developing your mindset is by increasing your skill set.

There is no secret to success; there is, however, a formula for success, and this is the blueprint:

1. Read up on your craft.

2. Invest in your education in that one laser-focused area by enrolling in relevant courses.

3. Attend live events such as seminars and conferences. Surrounding yourself with other like-minded individuals is extremely important to growth and development as well as networking and masterminding.

4. Find a mentor.

5. Market your product, service, course, or idea on social media.

6. Make more offers and convert those leads into sales.

Sounds simple right? According to American motivational speaker, Eric Thomas, "it's not easy, but it's simple." The path to success requires work, effort, drive, and determination; however, if you cover the hardest part, which is determining what it is you want to do, getting focused and executing the action will pay off in large dividends.

Let's do a quick exercise! I want you to create in your mind what the most successful person in your field looks like. Now ask yourself the following questions:

» What does this person do on a daily basis?

_____

_____

_____

» How early does their day start?

_____

_____

_____

» How do they generate leads?

_____

_____

_____

» What is their conversion rate?

_____

_____

_____

» What is their routine?

_____

_____

_____

» How many calls do they make?

_____

_____

_____

» Do they network?

_____

_____

_____

» What time does their day end?

_____

_____

_____

» What does success look like to me?

_____

_____

_____

» How much money do I want to earn?

_____

_____

_____

» How many clients, products or services do I need to sell to make this happen?

_____

_____

_____

» How soon do I want to make this money?

_____

_____

_____

Once you have all of the answers to these questions written down, guess what you have? A business plan for success.

So, now the only thing left to do is BECOME that person that you listed in the answers, and here's the great part about it; you can become that person as soon as YOU decide to become that person! I told you it's super simple!

One of the things my former managing broker told me was, "Jameka, you sure know how to fake it 'til you make it!" However, what she didn't know was I wasn't faking it; I already knew in real estate school that I was a successful real estate broker. As a matter of fact, before I completed the course, I told everyone that "I Am" in real estate before I even passed the test. "Why?" you ask. Because I believed in myself, and I knew I wasn't lying, I was prophesying; I call it "predictive programming!" Never doubt yourself, you will have potentially over 6 billion other people that will do that for you, so you have to bet on yourself to win!

You have to become your biggest cheerleader until you acquire fans, and that can only happen when you take action and make it happen! Do the thing that you dislike the most, first, whether it is phone calls, networking, or follow-ups but do something and do it consistently, and the law of averages will pay you for it after a while. Brian Tracy has a book called *Eat That Frog* which deals with overcoming procrastination and getting on with the hardest parts of your day first. Denzel Washington said in an interview, "Do what you got to do now, so you can do what you want to do later!" Surprise yourself with how great you can be, don't hold back, maximize your results with positivity and watch your bank account flow and personal self-esteem grow. You can do this but it really is all up to you. Henry Ford who only had a 4th-grade education and went on to become one of the world's leading car makers said, "If you think you can, you're right; if you think you can't, you're right."

So, there you have it, dear reader, you can choose to sit on the sideline and be an extra in your own movie, or you can choose to not only star in but also write and direct your own blockbuster major motion picture! Only you can decide, but I believe in you and the world is waiting on you to make moves!

What top 10 actions are you going to take in making your dreams come true?

1. _____
   _____
   _____
   _____
   _____

2. _____
   _____
   _____
   _____
   _____

3. _____
   _____
   _____
   _____
   _____

4. _____
   _____
   _____
   _____
   _____

5. _____
   _____
   _____
   _____

6. _____

_____

_____

_____

_____

7. _____

_____

_____

_____

_____

8. _____

_____

_____

_____

_____

9. _____

_____

_____

_____

_____

10. _____

_____

_____

_____

_____

_____

"

⁶ BUT LET HIM ASK IN FAITH, NOTHING WAVERING. FOR HE THAT WAVERETH IS LIKE A WAVE OF THE SEA DRIVEN WITH THE WIND AND TOSSED. ⁷ FOR LET NOT THAT MAN THINK THAT HE SHALL RECEIVE ANY THING OF THE LORD.

———

(JAMES 1:6-7 KJV)

"

7

CLARITY

Clarity means to be completely clear and lucid without any vagueness or ambiguity whatsoever. Having a great understanding of what you want and why you want it is an absolute must! Being clear in business, in your purpose, and in life is what true success looks like in a nutshell. Again, I have to be completely redundant when I say people don't get what they want because they truly don't know what they want. How can you expect to acquire anything when you're unsure? So, now this begs the question: how do I get crystal clear about my deeply innate desires? This is one of the hardest most thought-provoking questions ever asked but the good news is I'm going to help you with this!

Let's start here with a series of internal deep-diving reflections that are essential in activating your brain toward being brutally honest with yourself.

» If I knew there was absolutely no way I could fail, what profession would I be in?

_____

_____

_____

» If I had all of the money in the world and could travel anywhere in the world, where would I go?

_____

_____

_____

» What do I truly love doing when I find the time to do it?

_____

_____

_____

» What does true happiness look like to me?

_____

_____

_____

One of the most liberating exercises you can do has just been revealed to you. These provocative thought-inducing questions are invitations to open up your ability to dream again. It's a known fact that when you are under duress and stress concerning your everyday living, you're in fight or flight mode. There is a constant problem-solving frame of mind, a vortex if you will, that is suffocating all of your creativity and sentencing you to a lifetime of worry about bills. However, you are reading this book and I am now giving you permission to give yourself permission to look past your current circumstances and see the "you" that you know you truly are!

STUDY TO SHEW THYSELF APPROVED.

2 TIMOTHY 2:15 KJV

8

GROWTH

Immediately following my journaling session, which is jam-packed with reasons for my thankfulness and gratefulness, the next order of business is to have *"great fullness."* So yes, I made this word up but is it enough to just be thankful and that's it? No, the way I display my gratefulness is by learning to improve my skill set spiritually – I personally read my scriptures. It is the absolute best strategy for learning how to win overall in life, not in just one or two categories.

Directly after the scriptures, I read a minimum of 30 minutes to 1 hour on developing my skill set and mindset. I love reading autobiographies or biographical manuscripts that focus on people overcoming obstacles that were seemingly insurmountable, only to amass great fortunes and personal and professional achievements. Feel free to read whatever manuscript you believe in but make sure it uplifts you. There are great audio options that are available via Audible, podcasts, and the Clubhouse app. Additionally you can get some of your mindset training from personal development gurus like Jim Rohn, Brian Tracy, Tony Robbins, and one of my new favorites, Dr. Myron Golden, on YouTube, Facebook, Instagram, and LinkedIn.

It is vitally important and necessary to adhere to the knowledge and expertise of those that have gone before us because they can shave years off of your learning curve and help you avoid a lot of the pitfalls and mistakes that they've experienced. Most of them will tell you to be thankful for every experience, even the bad ones. The experts say that an attitude of gratitude is an important component of creating a healthy mindset and a wealthy bank account. I strongly suggest you heed their sage advice.

> *"This will be the third time I am coming to you. By the mouth of two or three witnesses every word shall be established."*
>
> **2 CORINTHIANS 13:1 NKJV**

Once the implementation of this simple adjustment in one's attitude commences, you will find your days more peaceful, joyful, and a new lust for life will spring forth before your very eyes. Improvement in your overall health and well-being is also inevitable.

Now, I want you to document the **top 10 things** you are thankful for. Write them down, and begin from this day forward, the daily practice of being thankful.

1. _____
   _____
   _____
   _____
   _____

2. _____
   _____
   _____
   _____
   _____

3. _____
   _____
   _____
   _____
   _____

4. _____
   _____
   _____
   _____
   _____

5. _____
   _____
   _____
   _____
   _____

6. _____
   _____
   _____
   _____
   _____

7. _____
   _____
   _____
   _____
   _____

8. _____
   _____
   _____
   _____
   _____

9. _____
   _____
   _____
   _____
   _____

10. _____
    _____
    _____
    _____
    _____
    _____

LET US HEAR THE CONCLUSION OF THE WHOLE MATTER.

ECCLESIASTES 12:13 NKJV

CONCLUSION:

GO FOR IT!

In my closing, I must congratulate you for taking the necessary steps in finishing this book. Success is inevitable as long as you have one primary result in all of your pursuits, which is to serve the people with integrity, honesty, and genuine care for their desired outcome, not yours. The famous motivational speaker and salesperson extraordinaire Zig Ziglar is quoted as saying, "If you help enough people get what they want, you will get what you want." I cannot tell you how many professionals have met early career destruction by "cutting corners." Not only have they lost their jobs, careers, families, and fortunes but they also ultimately wind up losing something so much more valuable in the marketplace, that is, a good reputation, and respect.

One must always remember that while embarking on your "Go For It" journey, do not lose your integrity, that is one thing that is not up for compromise. Many great men and women have fallen victim to the temptation of lying, cheating, and stealing to progress in life, and gain what they deem as getting ahead or even getting away with it, but the outcome never results favorably for those involved. The "Go For It" mentality is one of the highest virtues where you will aim to exemplify *Excellence, Intelligence, Opulence, and Affluence.* Dream Big, Think Big, Live Big, and you will have Big! Grant Cardone, one of the greatest real estate investors of our time, said "it's not go big or go home, it's go Big or go Bigger!" There is no place for you back there; your gaze is now set upward and onward, and you have all of the instructions on the "mind-training" necessary to make you a powerhouse in whatever vocation or profession you happen to be in.

Changing your mindset and gaining control of your thoughts on a day-to-day, minute-by-minute basis, by starting and ending your day with the preceding directives, will expedite your results in the most miraculous ways! Some people feel as though the speed at which many of their goals are achieved is like magic! I can vouch for the validity of those claims because I have reaped amazing achievements by consciously deciding to be prosperous as I excelled in my profession and even became an award-winning real estate broker in my first year!

So, I challenge you to surprise yourself, set the goals, write the vision, make the plans, chart your path to success, and watch them manifest before your very eyes. You owe it to yourself, to your family and to your community to become the absolute best version of yourself you can be. There is nothing for you to lose and everything for you to gain; Go Big, Go Forth and Go For It!

BIOGRAPHY

Jameka Jefferies is a full-time real estate broker and is the owner/CEO of her very own brokerage firm, Diamond Realty Partners, LLC. She has helped countless buyers and sellers reach their real estate goals and amass properties to enhance their financial portfolios. Her areas of specialty are first-time home buyers, commercial and luxury property sales. She has a passion to help educate and empower the community about the importance of wealth building, using credit responsibly, and amassing passive income through real estate.

Jameka is also the owner of Diamond Exotic Car Rentals, a high-end car rental company. With over 20 years of experience in sales and marketing, she has written real estate articles in the *New Haven Register* and has been featured on WTNH Ch 8 to give real estate tips for both buyers and sellers.

In 2019, she was chosen to be a panelist on the Rookie Rockstar forum for phenomenal first year sales of over 2 million. Additionally, she is an ordained minister, gospel singer/songwriter, sought-after motivational speaker, and television and radio host. Jameka has been invited on as a special guest for several national real estate and Christian podcasts.

Her first book entitled, *Take Your Life Back* (2009) was written to encourage women and to equip them with the necessary tools to rebuild after divorce and repair the brokenness that can result. That book was followed up by two informational real estate manuals on the home buying and selling process. Mrs. Jefferies believes that all things are possible to those who believe; Mark 9:23.

She currently resides in Connecticut with her loving husband Victor and three beautiful children. In her leisure time, she enjoys traveling, writing, and speaking.

You may reach her on social media:

- » Facebook page: Jameka Morrison-Jefferies

- » Instagram: jamekarealestate

- » Website: www.jamekaajeferries.com

www.ingramcontent.com/pod-product-compliance
Lightning Source LLC
Chambersburg PA
CBHW071501210326
41597CB00018B/2640